The Forbidden
Political Dictionary

The Forbidden Political Dictionary

Complete and Unapproved

JOHN CLIFTON

Illustrated by the Author

Foley Square

Publication date: April 1, 2010   ISBN 978-0-9760846-3-1

We encourage radio and television commentators to freely quote from this book on the air, but request that they source all quotes by mentioning the title and author.

Although the author and publisher have made every effort to ensure the accuracy and completeness of information contained in this book, we assume no responsibility for errors, inaccuracies, omissions or inconsistencies herein. Any slights of people, places, or organizations are unintentional.

Additional copies and information:
Visit the book's web site at *ForbiddenDictionary.com* for further information, and to order additional copies of this book. Also, you will find at the very end of this book a mail-in order form for purchasing more copies.

ATTENTION, CORPORATIONS, UNIVERSITIES, COLLEGES, AND PROFESSIONAL AND CHARITABLE ORGANIZATIONS: Quantity discounts are available on bulk purchases of this book for educational and gift purposes, or as premiums in fundraising efforts, etc. Inquiries should be addressed to:

Foley Square Books
P. O. Box 20548
Park West Station
New York, NY 10025
[212] 724-1578

Web: *FoleySquareBooks.com*
Email: info@FoleySquareBooks.com

"Dictionary, *n.* A malevolent literary device for cramping the growth of language and making it hard and inelastic. This dictionary, however, is a most useful work."
    – Ambrose Bierce,
    The Devil's Dictionary

The Seven Deadly Political Sins

COURAGE

CLARITY

GENEROSITY

CANDOR

SINCERITY

MODESTY

BREVITY

FOREWORD

*Y*ou are probably not reading this, since hardly anyone ever reads the foreword to any sort of book, let alone a dictionary. Nevertheless (Ahh, there's a good word!) forewords are demanded by editors and publishers in order to justify or apologize for the inability of the ensuing text to stand on its own without preliminary explanation.

The present volume (foreword-speak for "this book in your hand") being no real exception, I will attempt a modest introduction to this obviously ground-breaking (and heart-breaking) work of exceptional genius (I so characterize the book's quality in case you may not notice it).

I have always been a political junkie – you know, one of those people who actually follow the issues of the day, stay up late on election nights and buy newspapers solely for the editorials and the crossword puzzle. I've also been a longtime admirer of Ambrose Bierce's *The Devil's Dictionary*, from which this book obviously draws inspiration. What exactly are my politics? I hear you immediately ask. Well, I'm going to be coy on that one, since if I claimed a particular stripe, no one of the opposing viewpoint, tragically, would buy the book.

And I intend here an equal opportunity work as far as partisanship goes. If you are a ("raving") liberal or a ("staunch") conservative, or anything else, you will find, I trust, plenty with which to take exception within these covers. Politicians, after all, are really just one big happy family. They may regularly indulge in heated disagreements, partisan battles, mud-slinging skirmishes and occasional fisticuffs, but underneath, politicians are all the same – their underwear is cut from the same cloth, so to speak.

I've noticed over the years that while the right, left and center may vehemently differ on the issues, they all use the same words and phrases with which to excoriate each other and congratulate themselves. So words become the glue of politics (a comforting thought to think that our leaders are bound together in this way).

Therefore it was with a high-minded spirit I began to construct this compendium of political expression. I wanted to go beyond the mere standard dictionary definitions and probe beneath the words, exhuming the true meanings of the utterances of public figures. I don't refer to psychological meanings; in the first place I'm no shrink, and the inherent psychoses of politicians is already well documented. What I attempt here is simply to decode their messages. "Things are seldom what they seem," wrote W. S. Gilbert, and little did he know! In politics things are *never* what they seem, at least, so it seems. And, building on this unseemly thought, I began clarifying the everyday words and expressions one regularly encounters being bandied about in the political arena.

No doubt you might have a favorite that got left out, and for this (in the aforementioned spirit of the foreword) I apologize. All I can say is, I tried my best. Even the greatest lexicographers, I'm sure, make no claim of including absolutely everything possible. And, in my humble defense, let me point out that this is meant to be a handy portable reference – a book you might take around with you in your pocket, for ready use. You wouldn't want to carry a 10-pound tome around, would you? Sacrifices had to be made (I say this to cover up my inadvertent omissions as well – in true politician style).

And so, herein you will find, I hope, a good selection of terms, each duly defined (re-defined, I should say). In case you discover new, mind-opening meanings of familiar terms, forever changing your perception of certain words and phrases, I leave you with what little remains of the language after this book is finished with it.

I anticipate the accusation that the following is the work of a cynic, and readily accept it, considering cynicism one of the most necessary factors in maintaining a sane society (if there is such a thing). And, if you want to know what a cynic truly is, look it up – it's happily explained within.

Another matter some may find not to their taste is my tendency to avoid gender neutral language. It can get awfully tiresome trying to use substitutes for the male gender pronouns (he, him) in order to please readers sensitive to these things. Suffice it to say that, alas, I most often allowed readability to trump such awkward forms as "he/she" "him/her" and "congressperson." Sorry.

Finally, about the subtitle word "unapproved." Unapproved by whom? you might ask. Well, since I sought no approval for this work, I consequently got none. But I'm sure that disapproval of the book will be widespread, at least I hope so. General displeasure will ensure a large audience, if precedent is any indication.

Anyway, please use, read and refer to this book freely, with my approval.

— J. C.

A

academia, *n.* A cloistered community for the indoctrination of the young

academic, *adj.* Imaginary; hypothetical; hence, useless *n.* Theoretically, a hypothetical person (*See* scholar)

ACADEMIC

1

accord, *n.* An important diplomatic document signed by nations to cloak their mutual distrust

accountable, *adj.* Answerable to either your superior or the general public when your actions produce undesirable results. A private businessperson is automatically accountable since the marketplace is a fixed and visible measure by which one is assessed. Public officials are held accountable only if they fail to hide their misdeeds and are forced to confess, *i.e.* hardly ever.

activist, *n.* Busybody

adherent, *n.* A follower of a movement, individual, etc., so named for his inability to get unstuck from the movement, individual, etc.

advice and consent, *n.* Congressional approval of presidential appointments and treaties, the only constitutional power that Congress directly holds over the president short of impeachment, which is not to say the only power. For example, congressmen can ridicule a president's proposals or refuse to applaud at a State of the Union speech. However, they would thereby risk being uninvited to White House parties.

advisor, *n.* An official appointed to confirm the appointer's opinions

affirmative action, *n.* The opposite of "negative action" (the unfair repression of a minority), hence, the unfair advancement of a minority

2

Afghanistan, *n.* A country about which practically nothing is known and therefore constantly invaded

agent, *n. See* double agent

aggression, *n.* Pre-emptive defense *(q. v.)*; **aisle,** *n.* Unnecessary dividing line between Republicans and Democrats, redundant, since they're divided enough without it

ally, *n.* A person on your side in a particular conflict about a particular issue at a particular moment

ambassadorship, *n.* A reward for a significant presidential campaign contribution. Ambassadors work in foreign countries, so nobody is quite sure of or even interested in what they do.

amendment, *n.* Pork *(q. v.)*

American, *n.* Citizen of the United States of America, a country. While other countries may define their character by national tradition and history, Americans are brought together by TV sitcoms, their love of electronic gadgets and pop music. Depending upon their geographical locations, Americans love either cocktail parties or NASCAR events. Because the United States is so varied and diverse it is difficult to generalize about its people, since no matter what one may aver, someone will claim, often correctly, the opposite to be also true.

anarchist, *n.* One who supports (a) a country not being run by anyone, or (b) a country being run by anarchists

anti-, *prefix* Obnoxious in voicing opposition to, as in "anti-war," "anti-poverty," "anti-Christian," etc.

arms, *n.* The loudest and most convincing element of debate

assembly, *n.* Constitutional right to meet with subversives

astroturfing, *n.* Faked artificial grass roots effort actually instituted by seedy politicians, invariably hosed down and weeded out by the opposing party

authoritarian, *adj.* Popular; having wide appeal; destined to lead

avid, *adj.* Pathologically enthusiastic; irrationally obsessive, as an "avid follower," "avid party member," "avid reader," "avid admirer," etc.; insatiable; maniacal; greed-consumed

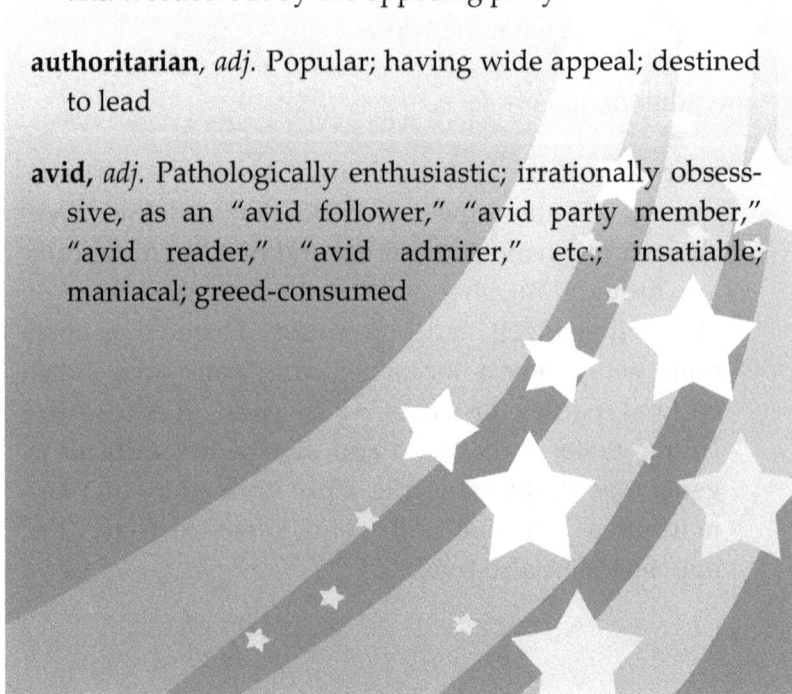

B

baby boomer, *n.* Member of a populous generation whose seminal influence was folk-rock lyrics

belittle, *v. t.* Speak of a colleague's recent accomplishment, award, victory, etc.

beltway, *n.* Circular line dividing governmental minds from the rest of the country's

beneficial, *adj.* Disastrous

benefits, *n. pl.* Goodies offered to make up for an unattractive job; **hidden benefit,** Something good you didn't even know you were getting

Bill of Rights, *n.* The first ten amendments to the U.S. Constitution, suggesting certain rights. Due to widespread historical ignorance, rights mentioned in the Bill of Rights are generally disregarded, while others, not specified, are assumed.

bleeding heart, *n.* Politician who appears to love the poor, the sick, the homeless and downtrodden in order to create sympathy for himself

blindside, *v. t.* Suddenly reveal a new approach

BLEEDING HEART

blog, *n.* Uncensored, unselfconscious, freely and cogently expressed Internet opinion piece written in haste and thus far superior to highly polished, overworked, over edited and overlong print articles.

Blue Dogs, *n .pl.* Conservative Democrats who argue with liberals until they are blue in the face, ultimately however, voting with them

book, *n.* Bound published material used for self-promotional and fundraising purposes. Having a book published enhances one's image regardless of the content, since very few will actually read it anyway.

border, *n.* An ignored line delineating the boundary between nations

budget, *n.* A plan detailing how taxpayer money is to be misspent

bully pulpit, *n.* A public platform provided to the highest ranking official for the purpose of leading the masses into something disagreeable

bureaucracy, *n.* A governmental office organized to employ the otherwise unemployable

bus, under the, *n.* Colorful phrase denoting a place to throw someone who has exceeded his/her usefulness to the point of being detrimental, preferred, for stylistic reasons, to expressions such as: "in front of the train," "onto the fire," "into the dumpster," "onto the guillotine," "in with the sharks," etc.

C

campaign ad, *n.* A commercial against a candidate

campaign manager, *n.* Overseer of operations with his eye on winning an election and subsequent appointment to a high office in the administration

Canada, *n.* An unimportant country to the north of the United States. Americans typically assume that Canada is mostly like the U.S., while in reality Canada is only something like the U.S. For example, Canadians call their states "provinces" and have very different and strange postal codes. When Americans think of Canada, they invariably call to mind their bacon, which they use in the preparation of Eggs Benedict. Another big difference between the two countries is that no Americans speak French.

candidate, *n.* An individual selected by an undisclosed person or anonymous group to run for office and do their bidding once elected

candor, in all, *n.* Phrase that precedes a lie or distortion

capital gains, *n.* The sometimes-felicitous result of financial risk, penalized by taxation

capital punishment, *n.* Finally executing a person who was sentenced to death so long ago that no one can recall who or why

8

capitalism, *n.* An as yet untried economic system in which wealth is created by individual enterprise and investment, free of interference from government

carbon footprint, *n.* Measurable total amount of carbon dioxide one creates while engaging in ecologically dangerous activities such as driving, cooking, bathing and breathing

caterwauling, *n.* Ambient sound of minority congressmen

cats and dogs, *n.* Bits and pieces of leftover impending legislation saved up for those slow days, the flotsam and jetsam of Congress, distinguished from, one imagines, the more important business of lions and tigers

celebrity, *n.* A well-known actor, sports figure, sex symbol, etc., whose political opinions are given great consideration by those who equate visibility with credibility

census, *n.* A population count conducted every ten years by volunteers with a stake in the outcome

centrist, *n.* One who rejects the left and rejects the right then combines the two

champion, *n.* Noisy advocate of a cause, group, etc.

charismatic leader, *n.* Dictator

9

CELEBRITY

charity, *n.* Organization whose executives are supported by donations, nominal portions of which are distributed to the needy

checks and balances, *n.* A system of self-regulating governmental power, whereby lawmakers take checks from their constituents thereby adding to their balances

cheerleaders, *n. pl.* Vocal devotees cultivated by leaders to create a false impression of wide support for a miserably conceived issue, proposal, etc.

China, *n.* Country whose body politic has a communist head and capitalist hands, discovered by Richard M. Nixon in 1972

clarify, *v. t.* Revise, as an ill-conceived, highly criticized remark you made recently

class, *n.* A section of a society distinguished by economic level (upper, middle, lower). A society with various classes is by nature diverse, while a classless society, by definition, lacks diversity. This presents a problem to socialists, who, oblivious to the paradox, insist upon both classlessness and diversity in their societies.

classic, *adj.* Shopworn; typical *Ex:* "His remarks were classic."

classified information, *n.* Knowledge found in the daily papers

cliché, *n.* Useful tool for an empty mind, enabling one to speak without speech's usual prerequisite, thought

climate change, *n.* Euphemism for "global warming" or "global cooling" used to frighten the person addressed when which of the two phenomena he supports is undetermined

cloakroom, *n.* The Capitol area where legislators meet, eat, chew the fat, etc., so called because discussions there are cloaked in secrecy, mystery, intrigue, etc.

cloture, *n.* Point at which legislators are sufficiently exhausted and hoarse to take a vote

11

co-, *prefix* Rival; competing; resented; as in "co-worker," "co-chair," "co-owner," etc.

coattail effect, *n.* Being in the right election at the right time, a phenomenon whereby a justifiably little known candidate can be elected because it was a good day for the party

colleague, *n.* Adversary; rival

collusion, *n.* Cooperation; unanimity achieved in private

colony, *n.* Working offspring supporting the family of the motherland

committee, *n.* A group assigned to work together on a certain task because none can be trusted to work alone

communism, *n.* A system of government by which poverty is shared equally

community organizing, *n.* Neighborhood improvement for political benefit

compassionate conservatism, *n.* Liberalism

competition, *n.* Combat; elimination of rivals

complex, *adj.* Describing an issue far above the listener's limited ability to understand and therefore not deserving an explanation (*See* weasel)

comprehensive, *adj.* Covering every area within one's limited scope

compromise, *n.* The result of two opponents lacking will

concerned, *adj.* Terrified

congress, *n.* 1. The act of coming together 2. A meeting of hostile participants; **United States Congress,** *n.* Body of wealthy citizens assigned to make laws for ordinary citizens without actually having to meet any

Congressional Record, *n.* Publication containing all business conducted on the floor of Congress, thereby a detailed account of half the story

connecting the dots, *n.* Process of relating random, insignificant facts in order to incriminate

consensus, *n.* Agreement by all members of a group brought about by pressure applied to dissenters

conservative, *adj.* Desiring change

conservative, *n.* One concerned with (a) what has worked in the past and (b) who is not working in the present

conspiracy theorist, *n.* Skeptic about whose ideas there is much skepticism. Some conspiracy theorists claim that Neil Armstrong did not walk on the moon, that the event was actually staged by Lee Harvey Oswald, although he did not act alone, in order to cover up the murder of Marilyn Monroe committed to stop the release of information about FDR's complicity in the attack on Pearl Harbor. Others rely upon imagination.

constituent, *n.* Resident in a politician's district with whom he makes contact just prior to elections

Constitution, *n.* The formative document of the United States, ratified in 1786, now mostly obsolete. Today, the Constitution is only cited when it contains affirmation of one's personal opinion and ignored when it conflicts with it.

context, *n.* Words that originally surrounded something quoted, which the quoted person can falsely claim were omitted intentionally, thereby creating a distortion

convention, *n.* Formerly, a coming together of a political party to nominate candidates. Currently, the coming together of a political party to have a political party

conventional wisdom, *n.* Anything widely regarded as true and therefore obviating any further investigation which might prove it false

core conviction, *n.* One's present fancy

core values, *n.* Values not subject to alteration, as contrasted with non-core values which, one surmises, are

corporation, *n.* A legal construction of persons, formed in order to relieve them of individual responsibility

corrupt, *adj.* Normal

counterterrorism, *n.* Killing, capturing, or making unflattering speeches about terrorists

creationist, *n.* One lacking the imagination required to believe in evolution

credit, taking, *v.* Thinking up someone else's good idea

crime, *n.* An act critical of society, occasionally resulting in punishment

crisis, *n.* Useful calamity

critique, *n.* **1.** Diatribe **2.** The trashing of an idea or person not to one's liking

cruel and unusual punishment, *n.* Punishment

cult, *n.* Extreme faction that believes, favors, or worships something or someone you find weird, unless it is something or someone you support

culture war, *n.* Struggle of the many differing social factions to dominate all the others

cynic, *n.* Perceptive person who sees falsity where others see truth and truth where others see falsity. Cynics are often deemed perverse, nasty souls, but are actually honest, nasty souls.

czar, *n.* A presidential advisor with far-reaching powers whose appointment is quietly announced on Friday evening

D

data, *n.* Information dug up and used to support a foregone conclusion

deal, *n.* Transaction in which all participating parties benefit and all non-participants are endangered

death penalty, *n.* Estate tax

debacle, *n.* A widely publicized political event or project

debate, *n.* A vicious quarrel among individuals competing for dominance

debt, *n.* The condition created when borrowed funds cannot be repaid because they've been spent on some worthless enterprise; **national debt**, Liability incurred by today's generation and to be paid back by tomorrow's; **bad debt**, Common redundancy, since there exists no good debt

defense, *n.* **1.** Protecting one's country against aggression. **2.** Aggression

deficit, *n.* The amount by which a government perpetually overspends each year

demagogue, *n.* Seeker of power who speaks loudly and with extreme emotion

DEAL

democracy, *n.* An obsolete system of government previously practiced in former cultures, most notably the United States of America. Under democracy, governments abided by the will of the people. Currently all people abide by the will of the government.

Democrat, *n.* A person not belonging to "any organized political party" (Will Rogers). Democrats were the invention of Andrew Jackson, later perfected by Franklin Delano Roosevelt. They were designed to create poverty programs, denigrate Republicans and save the world. They come in two basic models; the deluxe, which must be fueled with white wine and French brie, and the standard, which runs on canned malt beverages.

demonstration, *n.* Warning; an orchestrated threat

détente, *n.* In the game of war, a time-out

developing, *adj.* The state or quality of a country untouched by progress; undeveloped

dictator, *n.* A ruthless authoritarian despot who enslaves a country, highly regarded by celebrities

diplomat, *n.* Government official appointed to misrepresent his country

disarmament, *n.* Removing from yourself and your enemy the capability of self-defense. Obviously, any disarmament agreement that even one signatory violates subjects all others to an attack. Therefore disarmament destroys trust and increases vulnerability, creating the opposite of the intended effect.

disaster, *n.* Event which deters or delays one's sinister undertaking or secret plot; **manmade disaster**, New bureaucracy, law, economic plan, etc.; **natural disaster**, Nature's remedy for man's pretensions

discredit, *v. t.* To devalue a political rival through the release of irrelevant but unflattering facts, usually during an election campaign. (*See* knockout punch)

dissent, *n.* Disagreement, which is bound to appear no matter how excellent your idea, plan, or proposal may be, therefore necessitating preparations to squelch it even before revealing your idea, plan, or proposal

distortion, *n.* Almost a lie, but retaining enough truth to be believed, and thus more convincing than an outright far-fetched lie

District of Columbia, *n.* The seat of the United States government, both geopolitically and anatomically. Residents of the area, which is built on a swamp, are prohibited from voting in national elections, but are compensated for this by the honor of living close to politicians and tourists.

diversity, *n.* Variety of ethnicities, economic levels, ages, etc., highly prized by certain ideologues so long as there is no diversity in ideology

dog-whistle speech, *n.* An address containing code words with special meanings, only understood by others of the same breed

donation, *n.* Bribe

double agent, *n. See* agent

draconian, *adj.* Of or similar to the severe laws of Draco, an ancient Greek whose code punished even the most minor offenses by death. Since today hardly any offense is punishable by death (except in Texas), the use of this word to mean merely "stringent" or "strict" can only be characterized as hyperbole, another Grecian idea.

E

earmark, *n*. In a Congressional bill, a provision to provide provisions (*See* pork)

Earth Day, *n*. Annual outdoor celebration by ecology enthusiasts who gather to create environmental awareness and great quantities of litter

ecology, *n*. Study of God's scheme from man's point of view

economics, *n*. An unscientific science dealing with money, where it goes and how to prevent it from doing so; **supply-side economics**, Theory positing that by helping business, government helps the poor, since jobs are created and prices lowered. Detractors point out that businesses just pocket the cash without passing it on; **demand-side economics**, Theory positing that by helping the poor, government helps business, since people will have more money to buy stuff. Detractors point out that the poor just pay off overdue car payments or put the money under their mattresses without passing it on.

economy, *n*. A society's condition regarding the exchange of products and services, considered to be healthy by the majority party and ailing by the minority party. Economies, like children, are not considered healthy unless they are growing, but there is widespread disagreement on what to feed them.

20

educate, *v. t.* Convince

election, *n.* A public voting procedure whereby citizens select the wealthiest candidates

elite, *n.* On a typewriter, a font smaller than Pica; in society, a small group of pikers

elitist, *n.* One who is, by his own confession, more intelligent and privileged than everyone else

email, *n.* Electronic evidence revealing involvement in fraud, embezzlement and other crimes

eminent domain, *n.* A method for increasing tax revenues by replacing poor landowners with rich ones

employment, *n.* Reimbursed honest work, the last recourse for non-entrepreneurial types, non-heirs, non-retired, non-disabled, non-politicians and non-criminals

end of the day, at the, *n.* Hackneyed phrase replacing more original constructions such as "after all is said and done," "long story short," "bottom line," "in the final analysis," etc., etc.

enemy combatant, *n.* A trained foreign killer awaiting his court case

enemy, domestic, *n.* The opposing political party

enemy, foreign, *n.* A foreign country

energy conservation, *n.* **1.** Plan to produce as little energy as possible and use even less, resulting in a cleaner environment and a lower standard of living **2.** Importation of oil, gas, etc.

enlightened, *adj.* Converted to one's own philosophy

entente, *n.* Truce agreement; period of unease

entitlement, *n.* According to Republicans, a government giveaway entitling one to the earnings of others, creating a class of legal pickpockets. As defined by Democrats, a compassionate transfer of wealth from their enemies to their supporters

entrepreneur, *n.* One who benefits humanity by providing goods or services so desirable that people are willing to pay for them, widely distrusted by socialists

equal, *adj.* Subject to the same failures and disappointments as others

espionage, *n.* Surveillance activities carried out by governments on foreign countries and domestic taxpayers

estimate, *n.* Undercalculated cost of a proposed new program, project, entitlement, war, etc.

ethics, *n.* A code of behavior that public servants must appear to follow

euro, *n.* Common unit of currency created to reduce competition among European countries in order to better compete with non-European countries

evidence, *n.* Unwelcome facts

evil, *n.* Obsolete concept mistakenly ascribing deleterious acts to a universal malevolent power instead of the correct source, societal victimization

evolution, *n.* The belief that God created man in many incremental steps over an astronomically long period of time

ESPIONAGE

exceptional, *adj.* Not normal; unusual, such as a kept promise or something not made in China

exceptionalism, American, *n.* Credo, confirmed by immigration figures, that the United States is not the same as Uzbekistan

exit poll, *n.* A list of questions asking who one voted for and why, which may be answered truthfully or not, used to determine election outcomes prematurely

exit ramp, *n.* A plan for an accelerated escape from your jalopy of a proposal in case, down the road, it backfires or runs out of gas

exit strategy, *n.* Message to the enemy explaining just how you will surrender

expert, *n.* A person who has written a book

exploit, *v. t.* Employ, utilize

extortion, *n.* Popular fundraising technique; taxation

F

fact, *n.* Argument stopper, often, but not always, as when an opponent is left unimpressed with or confused by one

faculty lounge, The quintessential location for academic blather, except for, of course, the classroom

fair, *adj.* Favorable to one side, as in "fair trade," "fair employment," etc.

fairness doctrine, *n.* A scheme wherein speech is censored and/or controlled on the basis of even-handedness as determined arbitrarily

fallacy, *n.* Element in an opponent's argument with which you disagree

fanatic, *n.* Dedicated person scorned for his enthusiasm. Noted fanatics in history include John the Baptist, Copernicus, Michelangelo, Gandhi, Joan of Arc, Galileo, Malcolm X and Jesus Christ. Society's typical treatment of fanatics consists of (in chronological order): amusement, mockery, excoriation, persecution, execution. Occasionally, fanatics escape this sequence and become history's respected authorities.

farce, *n.* A major ambitious undertaking by an opposing faction

far-sighted, *adj.* Having an inability to correctly observe the present situation

fascist, *n.* One who believes that the state should control production, as distinguished from a liberal, who believes that the state should control everything

Federal Reserve, *n.* One of the four branches of government (Executive, Legislative, Judicial and Federal Reserve), whose function is to print too much money

federal, *adj.* Anything to do with the national government, usually unworkable, unaffordable, unnecessary or unconstitutional

feet, on one's, *n. pl.* **1.** In the posture and movement of a pugilist. One "good on his feet" is adept at spontaneously dodging or returning embarrassing verbal blows or difficult truths from opponents. **2.** Where one is said to land after successfully suppressing a potentially devastating knockout from a scandal, inquiry, indictment, etc.

feminism, *n.* The glorification of women and things female, a prevalent practice among male chauvinists *See* sexism.

fence mending, *n.* A futile meeting with one's constituents in order to smooth over their disapproval of your recent votes

filibuster, *n.* A legislative trick employing verbal cartwheels, rhetorical somersaults and emotional handstands in order to stand a vote on its head

FARSIGHTED

fishing expedition, *n.* A congressional hearing trying to discover the nefarious reason for which it is being held

flag, *n.* A country's banner revered by the patriotic and scorned by the college educated

flexibility, *n.* Wishy-washiness; ability to easily bend, especially from the waist

flyover country, *n*. American heartland, rarely visited by coastal elites, thus an area of great distinction

focus group, *n*. A small collection of non-entities whose opinions are solicited in order to decide important national issues

founding father, *n*. Discredited or obscured figure suspected of contributing to the origin of the United States

Frankenstein monster, *n*. (*slang*) Piece of major legislation

free enterprise, *n*. Commerce which is unbounded and unrestricted, seldom seen except as criminal enterprise

freedom of choice, *n*. License to select something disparaged

freedom, *n*. Permission to do what is permitted

friend, *n*. A person you have met; **dear friend**, Someone you had dinner with; **close friend**, Wealthy constituent, regular customer; **best friend**, Co-conspirator

fundraiser, *n*. A political event where stomachs are filled and pockets are emptied

future, *n*. **1.** Distraction from a present debacle upon which we must now focus, as suggested by the creator of the debacle **2.** Hopeful tomorrow when today's misfortunes and follies are mistakenly assumed to be vanquished

G

Gaia, *n.* Euphemistic deity, used where "God" would be awkward in explaining the Creation

gerrymander, *v. t.* To draw the outline of an election district with a fresh, creative, non-geometric approach

gift, *n.* A self-damaging error made by a rival

give and take, *n.* Willingness to barter one's beliefs and opinions

global warming, *n.* **1.** A religion that declares man, not Satan, to be the source of evil **2.** Term used to mask the earth's gradual cooling **3.** Actual warming of the globe

globalism, *n.* A movement to universalize governmental ineptitude and eliminate choice. Presently, if one doesn't like living under the government in Uganda, he can move to Spain or Australia. Under globalism, he might as well stay in Uganda.

Good Neighbor Policy, *n.* Guidelines specifying that the United States will not have anything to do with South America

good, *adj.* Benefiting one's self-interest; helpful in advancing one's plan to dominate

government program, *n.* A central plan introduced to correct the deleterious effects of an existing one

government, *n.* Controlling authority of a nation, state, city, etc., paid for by the People. Authoritarian governments are effectively compact in size, while democratic governments come in various sizes, running from "large" to "extra large" to "too damn large."

Great Society, *n.* Utopia; dream

guideline, *n.* Someone else's plan for your course of behavior

guilt, *n.* Feeling of culpability cultivated in one's enemies in order to weaken their resolve and thus gain the upper hand

gun control, *n.* Misnomer for "gun-owner control." Opponents of gun control argue that guns prevent crime, while advocates claim that guns cause crime. Legal gun owners live in rural areas of southern states, while illegal gun owners live in large northern cities.

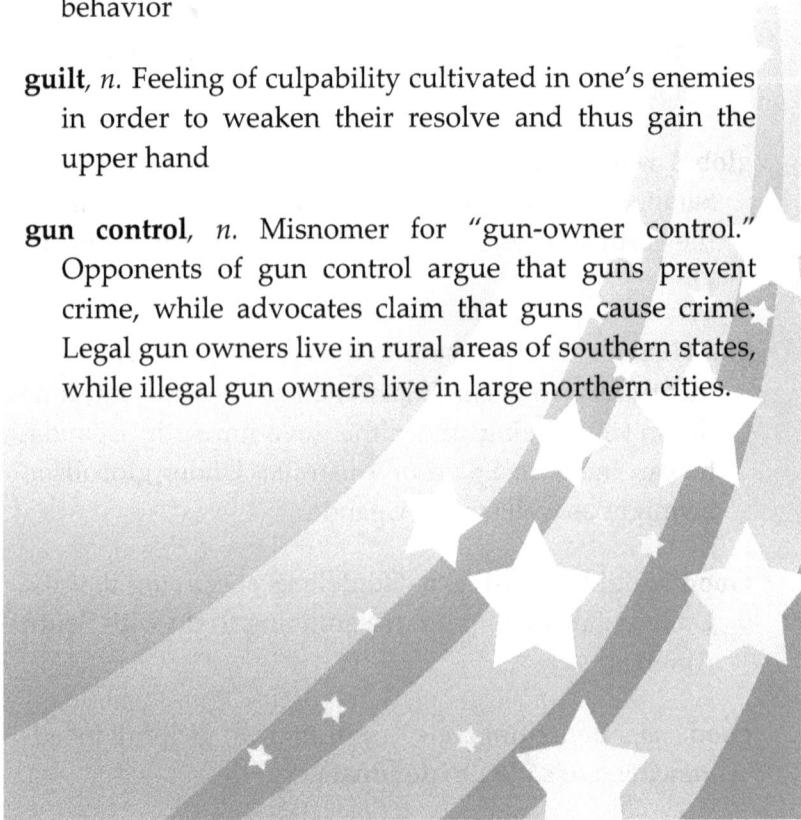

H

half a loaf, *n*. A loser's winnings

hardball, *n*. Speech or action without the frills of propriety, decent language, respect, etc.

hate crime, *n*. Any crime involving two offenses, one of which is hate. Since hate by itself is never a punishable offense, a hate crime is therefore a single offense subject to two punishments

hate speech, *n*. Activity one can accuse adversaries of participating in when you either (a) haven't heard what they said, or (b) disagree with their politics. Since hate is universally disapproved of, accusing another of it is invariably a surefire way to weaken support for the person, especially if you cannot cite specific quotes of what was said.

hearing, *n*. An opportunity for congressmen to severely chastise individuals they call before them for this purpose

Hispanic vote, *n*. The part of the electorate that speaks Spanish, erroneously considered a uniform bloc, but actually comprising many various political views, unless the candidate is Hispanic

historian, *n*. One who edits history

31

history, *n.* The long line of past events that has produced the present mess

hoax, *n.* False, misleading event which, however, reveals the truth about those who fall for the deception, therefore a very useful tool in exposing a reality by means of an unreality

HEARING

home schooling, *n.* Demonstrably superior teaching method, consequently frowned on by educators and teachers' unions

homeland security, *n.* Protection of a country, necessitated by border insecurity

homeless, *n.* Section of society consisting mainly of people formerly called "bums" or "hoboes," preferring the freedom of the street to the squalor of government housing or facilities. Other homeless are mental incompetents forced out of institutions by civil liberties advocates and forced into overnight shelters by police. The "plight of the homeless" is a perennially favorite topic of the party out of power, but no actual action is ever taken.

horrific, *n.* Overused description of something accurately defined as horrendous, horrifying, appalling, shocking, ghastly, sickening, disgusting, gruesome, deleterious, awful, nasty, wicked or horrible (*See* Roget)

hypocrisy, *n.* Broadmindedness which embraces the condoning of two opposite behaviors, one exhibited in public and the other in private; a tolerant and enlightened meld of the outwardly moral and inwardly immoral in one personality

I

ideologue, *n.* One who knows why he must do something, but has no idea how to do it

immigration reform, *n.* A plan to eliminate illegal residents of a country by declaring them legal residents of a country. (*See* Democrat)

impeachment, *n.* Repayment by Congressmen for disrespect shown to them by a president, which they characterize as high crimes and misdemeanors

incident, *n.* Embarrassing event

inclusive, *adj.* Appealing to many likeminded individuals

incremental, *n.* Happening by small degrees so as to go unnoticed, as a tax hike, war escalation, etc.

incumbent, *n.* Election winner; permanent office-holder

Independent, *n.* One claiming very strong political beliefs and therefore not suitable for party membership

inflammatory, *adj.* Critical

infrastructure, *n.* The physical foundations of a society, such as roads, bridges, cell phones and Twitter

injustice, *n.* Result of not getting one's way

IDEOLOGUE

insider, *n.* One whose bad side is outside of oversight

insurrection, *n.* A movement against authority which the authority stamps out, thus adding to its power and prestige

integrity, *n.* Affected prudence mistaken for virtue

intellectual, *n.* One whose job is to think instead of work. After communist revolutions intellectuals are the first to go, since communists want workers, not thinkers. Consequently, communist intellectuals always reside in non-communist countries such as America, where all intellectuals are graduates of Harvard.

intelligence, *n.* Many bits of data, individually insignificant, but when combined revealing a mystifying picture

interim appointment, *n.* Sale of a vacated office

Internal Revenue Service, *n.* A public agency about the inner workings of which nothing is known, assigned to collect taxes by any means necessary

interrogation tactic, *n.* Method of persuading a detainee to say something

investigation, *n.* An inquiry into the actions of one's enemy

investment, *n.* **1.** Money speculated in hope of a financial gain **2.** Tax (*See* Congress) **3.** Government spending project (*See* pork)

issue, *n.* Brouhaha

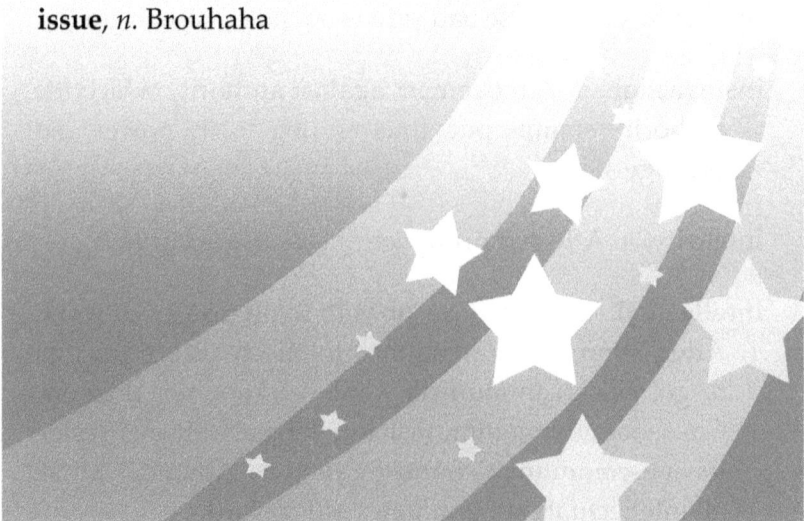

J

jackass, *n.* Person who questions your position, integrity, honesty, intelligence, etc.

Jacobin, *n.* French democrat; terrorist

jam, *n.* Between a rock and a hard place, as when a legislator, in the spotlight of the media, tries to please his colleagues as well as his constituents while not opposing the president or making a statement that can be quoted out of context

JUNKET

jaundiced, *adj.* Quality of a highly discerning eye cast upon a ridiculous suggestion

jejune, *adj.* Combining youthful ignorance with a lack of spark

jihad, *n.* An Islamic movement whose goal to achieve worldwide membership eschews gentle persuasion

jobs program, *n.* Public sector plan to create employment with money taken from the private sector, thereby creating a net gain of zero jobs while increasing popular support from the unemployed

junket, *n.* An official government fact-finding trip to study Barbados or Las Vegas

justice, *n.* The servant of revenge

K

K Street, *n.* Avenue in Washington, D. C. populated with lobbyists, hence Washington's Main Street

kangaroo court, *n.* A contentious showy trial, so-called because of the animal's boxing prowess and the fact that the outcome is in the pocket

kerfuffle, *n.* A highly damaging or incriminating affair depicted as a minor superficial incident, *i.e.* "The embezzlement kerfuffle," or "the adultery kerfuffle." (*See* brouhaha)

key witness, *n.* Unindicted criminal accessory

Keynesian, *adj.* Following an economic plan originally devised to end the Great Depression, apparently much admired, since it was relied upon for fully nine years until the Depression ended

keynote address, *n.* At a political event, the most important and interminable speech

kickback, *n.* Reward; token of appreciation, usually unpublicized

kill, *v .t.* Terminate another's career, legislative effort, candidacy, romantic relationship, marriage and/or reputation

king of the hill, *n.* Amendment rule favoring the House amendment with more votes than other amendments, as amended

king, *n.* The best, worst or most prominent in a particular field, as in "billiards king," "king of double-speak," "spending king," "king of the half-truth," etc.

kingmaker, *n.* The individual behind the success of someone, both before and after the success. King-makers throw an individual into the arena and then remain as the power behind the thrown.

kiss of death, *n.* A demolishing nicety

kleptocracy, *n.* Government by those who seek personal gain at the expense of the governed, hence, government

KEYNOTE ADDRESS

40

knee-jerk, *adj.* Automatically reflexive; thoughtlessly opinionated; said mainly of liberals, mostly because conservatives favor the term more highly, liberals preferring "Neanderthal" or "troglodyte"

knockout punch, *n.* Secret destructive information the revealing of which one saves for the end

know-how, *n.* Mistaken belief in one's ability

known, *adj.* Supposed; **known fact,** *n.* Rumor; **known suspect,** *n.* Disliked person; **known quantity,** *n.* Estimate

knucklehead, *n.* Alternate pejorative term for the more proper "birdbrain." (*See* pinhead, clown, bozo, jerk, screwball, *etc.*)

kosher, *adj.* Conforming to one's personal code of behavior

Kool-Aid, *n.* The sugary drink symbolizing blind acceptance of a doctrine. To "drink the Kool-Aid" means to believe unquestioningly till the death, as did the members of the religious cult from whence the phrase originated. What seems to be forgotten is that the beverage was laced with poison and that it killed the drinkers immediately. Actually, then, the phrase means to believe unquestioningly in something that will kill you, namely the doctrine, not very flattering to the doctrine.

kowtow, *v, i.* To fall in line, knowing on which side one's bread is buttered

41

L

labor union, *n.* A group of workers organized to obtain more and more pay for less and less work, the ultimate objective being infinitely high wages for absolutely no work.

laissez faire, *adj.* A French system by which people are generally uncontrolled, therefore a system totally incomprehensible to modern democracies

lame duck, *n.* One voted out but still not quite out of office, not having two legs to stand on, but still quacking

lawyer, *n.* One versed in litigation and skilled in prevarication who represents clients and misrepresents facts in order to beat the law

laying on the table, *n.* **1.** Merciful act of ending debate **2.** Obscene act in the office

leader, *n.* Troublemaker

leadership, *n.* The ability to convince a follower that he is wrong

leak, *n.* Anonymous spilling of the beans, the mother's milk of the press

LEAK

liar, *n.* Person plainly worse than one who "exaggerates," "prevaricates," "dissembles," "distorts," or "plays havoc with the truth." Flatly calling another a liar is considered the severest of insults, particularly when it is a provably accurate statement.

liberal, *adj.* Excessive, as in a "liberal" helping of ice cream

43

liberal, *n.* One who rejects the tried and true in favor of the untried and untrue

libertarian, *n.* One who maintains that nothing should be illegal except non-libertarian positions

liberty, *n.* Type of independence not quite as preferable as "freedom," due to its observation of self-control and respect for the liberty of others

librarian, *n.* Administrator of a literary collection and staunch opponent of censorship, insisting that all have the right to borrow pornography as long as it is returned by the due date

limited monarchy, *n.* The British royal family, although some of its members are more limited than others

line-item veto, *n.* A powerful tool whereby a president may cross out repulsive parts of an otherwise merely odious bill. Passage of a line-item veto measure is perennially proposed on the grounds that it will reduce pork spending; thus it remains a hopeless fantasy

lobbyist, *n.* In legislative bodies, the final authority

logic, *n.* **1.** The enemy of persuasion **2.** Ineffective and unconvincing element of an argument, as opposed to emotion, the final arbiter

logrolling, *n.* Conspiracy between two legislators to vote for each other's home state pork bill, as in "Cast your vote my way and I'll vote for your highway."

M

Mafia, *n.* Political action group with a unique code of morality

mainstream, *adj.* Of the nameless, faceless, undefined masses, as opposed to the visible, identifiable minorities, as in "mainstream opinion" or "mainstream thought"

mandate, *n.* Misreading of the meaning of an election

mantra, *n.* Statement deemed true by virtue of its multiple repetitions

marriage, *n.* **1.** Religious sacrament joining a man and a woman in matrimony **2.** Civil procedure joining anyone with whatever the law allows. Many advocates of the separation of church and state inexplicably also favor the mixing of a church sacrament (marriage) with a state ceremony (civil union). Also, many heterosexuals favor homosexual marriage, feeling it only equitable that their matrimonial misery be shared by all.

Marxist, *n.* Communist who never has lived in a communist country

mea culpa, *n.* Latin phrase indicating defiant pride in one's misdeeds

mendacity, *n.* The official language of power

mentality, *n.* State of mind; preconception; stupidity; **entitlement mentality**, Notion that the wealthy, and not you, got rich off your back; **sixties mentality**, Fixation on revolution, weed, and tie-dyed shirts; **tax-and-spend mentality**, Compulsion to give the public unsolicited gifts, paid for with their own money; **far right mentality**, Belief that wearing fur is still OK; **"me" mentality**, Self-pride in the self-interest of self-gratification; **Cold War mentality**, Persistence in calling Russia the "Soviet Union"

SIXTIES MENTALITY

46

message, *n.* A politician's shtick included in his/her act; **on message**, *adj.* Repeating the same phrases incessantly; **off message**, *adj.* Inadvertently spontaneous

middle ground, *n.* No-man's land between two ideas, containing the drawbacks of both and the advantages of neither

militia, *n.* Armed citizen groups organized for or against a government

mindset, *n.* Incurable brain condition

minimum wage, n. The absolute lowest amount that one's labor is worth, often disagreed upon by the employer and the employee. Fortunately, government rescues the situation by setting an arbitrary figure.

Miranda rights, *n.* Rights of an arrestee to remain silent, engage a lawyer, and wear a tutti-frutti hat

mistake, *n.* One of an endless series of repetitions of a particular error; **mistakes**, *n. pl.* Actions, such as crimes, infidelities, frauds, corruptions, lies, etc., that a discredited or disgraced person claims to have made in the past, as in "I have made many mistakes."

misunderestimate, *v.* According to George W. Bush, a president, to misoverestimate how little there is

moderate, *adj.* Confused

moderate, *n.* One having neither conservative nor liberal convictions, hence, one having no basis upon which to form an opinion

mole, *n.* Our enemy spy planted among their enemy spies, masquerading as a spy for the enemy

monopoly, *n.* A country run by a single government (*See* anarchy)

moral clarity, *n.* The exact mirror of one's own views

moral, *adj.* Approved

motor voter, *n.* Curious process that links driving with voting, a drive-by registration. Interestingly, applicants for driver's licenses might also be offered an accompanying voter's registration, but applicants for voter registration are never offered an accompanying driver's license.

muckraker, *n.* Journalist

multiculturalism, *n.* Overuse of hyphenation (*See* diversity)

N

nationalism, *n.* A rating system by which one's own country automatically scores higher than others

nation-building, *n.* Process whereby a country is destroyed in order to replace it with another one more desirable to the builder

NATO, *n.* An alignment of nations pledging mutual protection against the memory of the Soviet Union

Nazi *n.* **1.** Epithet applied to political enemies **2.** Actual member of the "National Socialist German Workers' Party" *(National-sozialistische Deutsche Arbeiterpartei)*, a mid-twentieth century movement responsible for the Holocaust

negotiate, *v. t.* To give an enemy what he wants

neocon, *n.* Conservative not to the manner born

New Deal, *n.* A refreshing of one's hand in a game of chance, hence a fresh plan with an unforeseen outcome

news media, *n.* The vehicles (print, electronic, etc.) which repeat and disseminate stories they get from wire services and Internet blogs. Some opine that the news media are biased; others say prejudiced, while others sympathetically claim they are brain dead. Still others excuse the media as being merely lazy.

news, *n.* Editorialized account of events. The traditional rules for writing a news story are to answer the following: (1) WHO did such a stupid thing? (2) WHAT did they think they were doing? (3) WHERE were their brains? (4) WHEN did they stop using common sense? (5) WHY are they still walking the streets?

NEWS

non-partisan, *adj.* Agreed to by one's own party and therefore obviously the right choice for the other party

nonprofit, 1. *adj.* Failing 2. *n.* Phony company run by an office-holder's spouse or sweetheart used to launder funds

nuance, *n.* Slight difference that makes all the difference

nuclear, *adj.* Possessing the radically devastating effect of a bomb, as a new procedure in the House, severe political tactic, Supreme Court decision, resignation, announcement, accusation, repeal of an entitlement, etc.

O

obfuscation, *n.* The first language of the public arena

obscene, *adj.* Hideously detestable, describing such things as congressional bills, proposals, ideas, speeches, persons, etc.

obsequious, *adj.* Overly fond or subservient; typified by the lavish honoring of a live person as if he were dead

obsession, *n.* Devotion; singleness of purpose; concentration

obtuse, *adj.* Quality of a skull's high density and low penetrability

obvious, *adj.* Easily noticed, as another's mistake

October surprise, *n.* Release of information just before election day that you offered a bribe to silence an informer who was about to reveal that you had a drunken adulterous affair twenty years ago while driving 85 miles per hour in a 45 m.p.h. zone with no license after leaving the Pink Pussycat Café with a topless dancer in Casper, Wyoming

off the mark, *adj.* Conflicting with one's own view

OCTOBER SURPRISE

off year, *n.* A period when there is no imminent election, hence a time of irresponsible political actions which will be forgotten by re-election time

oligarchy, *n.* Government by the few, *i. e.* without the frills of bureaucracies, legislative bodies, laws, courts, etc.; a prime example of the fallacy "less is more."

onus, *n.* Burden of responsibility deflected from oneself to one's opponent

opportunist, *n.* Politician

53

optimist, *n.* One who sees the future as it could be if we would all just make an effort

outreach, *n.* The act of extending hands to others in order to control them

ownership, *n.* What is left to you when others run for the hills after an ambitious plan you championed has turned into a fiasco

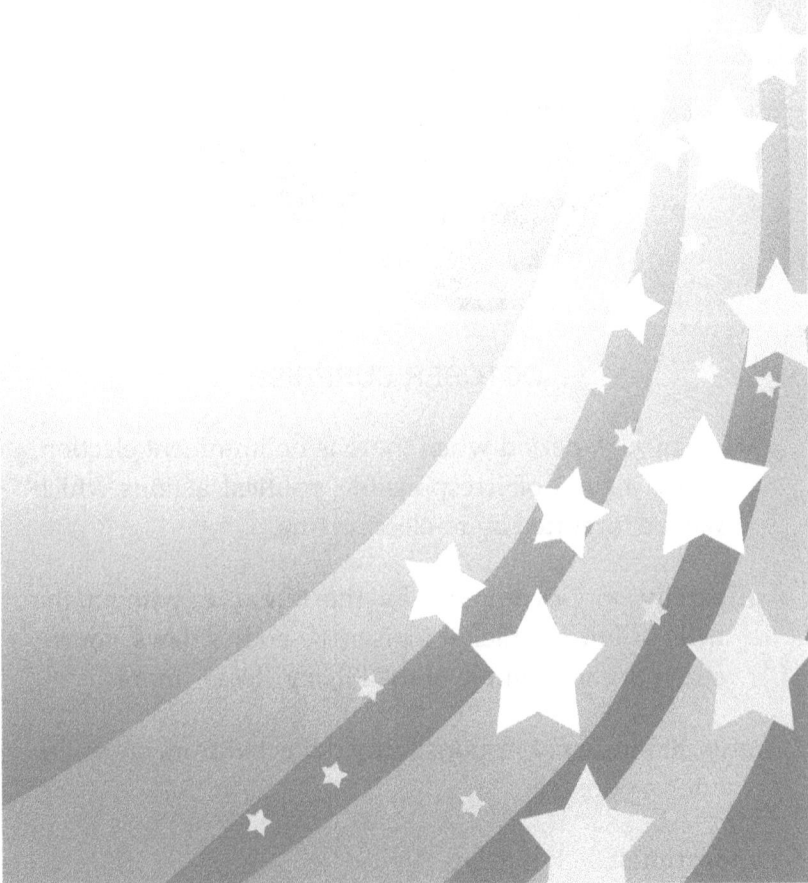

P

pacifist, *n.* One who would not participate in violent conflict, but would participate in violent protest

pander, *v. i.* To opine your audience's opinions

panel, *n.* A group of television commentators all of the same political stripe except one, who is included for the appearance of balance

paper trail, *n.* Series of documents constituting a provable record of one's actions, highly valuable in defending oneself or attacking another

paraphrase, *v. t.* Plagiarize

parse, *v. t.* To choose words carefully, so that they will be more easily misunderstood

partisan, *n.* **1.** A party animal, most commonly a donkey or elephant, hence inhuman **2.** Member of the opposition party who will not cooperate

pathetic, *adj.* Description of an antagonist's response to one's incisive analysis

patriot, *n.* A person grateful to his country, due to lack of sufficient cynicism

peace process, *n.* Diplomacy sticking its nose in where it's not wanted

peace, *n.* Brief period between two wars

peer review, *n.* A worthless fact check on a scientist's publicized data by another scientist. When two scientists disagree with each other, both endeavor to have the other's findings discredited through this process, invariably resulting in a stalemate of professional animosity and public exasperation.

peer, *n.* Individual equal to oneself, normally encountered while on jury duty

perfidy, *n.* The act or quality of being disloyal, normally considered contemptible, but in politics a virtue

perk, *n.* *(slang)* Perquisite. Additional salary an employer pays not in money but in the form of goods or services so as to reduce his taxes and overhead while making himself seem generous to employees. (*See* win-win)

pessimist, *n.* One who sees the future as it most surely will be if we're not careful

photo-op, *n.* Fake event staged for the explicit purpose of producing self-promotional photographs, one of the distinct situations in which politicians actually encourage the taking of candid pictures

PLAGIARISM

plagiarism, *n.* Creative writing with creative authorship. The most highly skilled plagiarists copy from forgotten, even ancient, sources, making it less likely that the true author will be recognized. Experts in the practice frequently rewrite, translate and/or paraphrase the original, the better to disguise it as new work. Successful plagiarists are by definition not recognized as such, since they have been so proficient in the practice they go undetected. The very finest plagiarists are recognized as great writers, sadly never gaining recognition for their greatness as plagiarists.

Pledge of Allegiance, *n.* An oath of fidelity to flag and country recited by schoolchildren to introduce new vocabulary words, such as "nation," "republic," "liberty," "God," etc. Many students often question the identity of "Richard Stans," ("and to the republic for Richard Stans"), why the nation is "invisible" and why it's "just us" for all and not everyone.

pledge, *n.* A carelessly conceived and unsupported guarantee, usually preceded by "solemn"

policy, *n.* A published set of directives used to hide an unpublished set of directives

political correctness, *n.* A code of restricted behavior and speech created by those who consider themselves fortunate to conceal their contempt for those they consider unfortunate, thereby appeasing the guilt of the fortunate for being fortunate

political suicide, *n.* Rare act in which a public servant does the right thing even though it dooms his re-election, which often is also the right thing

politics, *n.* **1.** The only science involving mass opinion, hence the most popular **2.** The art of government, pejoratively **3.** Querulous stumbling block to progress

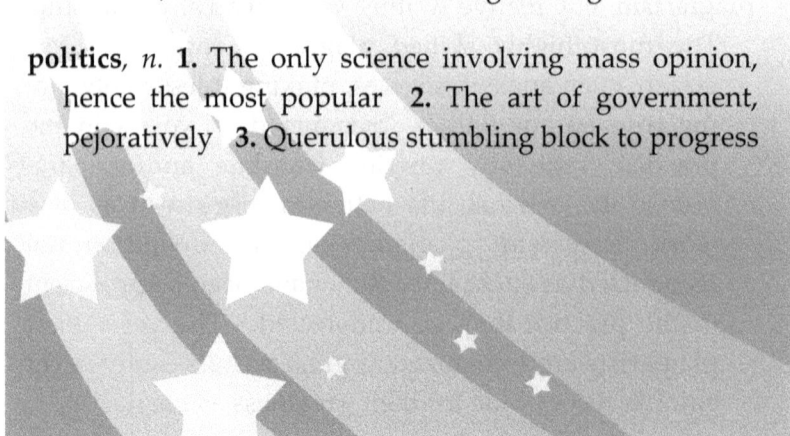

politics, playing, *n.* Topic one rules out of the discussion when a member of the opposing party accuses one or one's party of a major blunder. In such cases the member of the blundering party accuses the attacker of "playing politics," thereby taking the high ground over his own party's screw-up. This is followed up with "The main thing is to fix the problem, not make this a petty political issue."

poll, *n.* A survey to determine popular opinion on a topic, candidate, etc., the outcome of which is determined by the wording of the questions

population control, *n.* **1.** Effort to reduce human resources in order to increase natural resources **2.** Tyranny **3.** War **4.** Smoking

pork, *n.* Fat used by congressional hogs to lard a bill in order to bring home the bacon (*See* amendment)

portray, *v.* Depict or describe an adversary as possessing your faults

poverty line, *n.* An arbitrary line set by politicians below which you are poor and above which you are rich. This line is usually set high, insuring that more people are deemed poor, the better for government to subsidize them and thus gain their vote

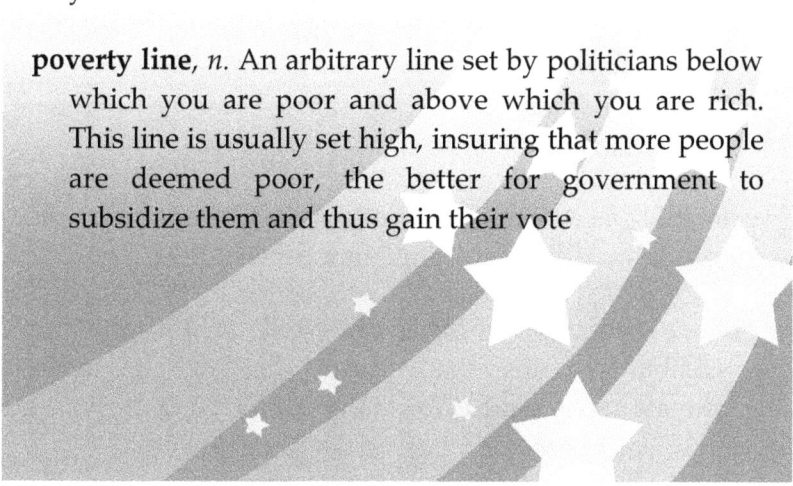

power grab, *n.* Seizing control over an area or entity hitherto unregulated. To effect a power grab, the following sequence is recommended: (a) Call attention to a particular industry or structure. (b) Convince the electorate that it is a terrible mess, inefficient, corrupt, etc. (c) Impress upon all that you are the best one to repair the situation and, though it would be a great sacrifice, would begrudgingly accept control. (d) Modestly accept responsibility and eliminate present controlling personnel. (e) Build a new, self-perpetuating bureaucracy around yourself. (f) After a while, when no improvement is discernable, blame your predecessors.

pragmatist, *n.* One who gets things done, but can't say why

precedent, *n.* In law, a mistake made in a previous case and therefore followed in subsequent cases

predecessor, *n.* Previous holder of an office whose successes are forgotten and whose failures are remembered

primary, *n.* Largely ignored election of secondary interest and tertiary attendance

principle, *n.* A conviction, often abandoned upon the adoption of another, conflicting conviction

private sector, *n.* Antithesis of "public sector," the two combining to form the "great divide." Activities in the private sector tend to be made public, while activities in the public sector are generally kept private.

pro life, *adj.* Believing by choice that life begins at conception; **pro choice,** *adj.* Believing in the conception that life ends by choice

pro tem, *adj.* Holding a position or office just for the time being, but too long nonetheless

pro-, *prefix* Violently or excessively approving of, as in "pro-labor," "pro-war," pro-marriage," "pro-death penalty," etc.

probe, *n.* Investigative procedure initiated to empower the investigator and weaken the investigated; **probed,** *adj.* Screwed

progress, *n.* Accomplishment, as in silencing a detractor or achieving an undeserved success

progressive, *n.* Member of a movement that abandons the mistakes of the past for the mistakes of the future

projection, *n.* **1.** TV election night prediction of a race's outcome made by a network early enough to keep you from checking another channel and late enough to avoid being embarrassingly wrong (*See* exit poll) **2.** Accusing a member of another party of committing a reprehensible act you and your party are famous for

proliferation, *n.* The fruitful increase and flowering of ideas, populations, nuclear weapons, etc.

promise, *n.* Lie

propagandist, *n.* Writer, speaker, broadcaster, etc.

property, *n.* Personal possession not yet confiscated by government

protest, *n.* Dissent expressed in one of two formats, i.e. organized protest or spontaneous protest, the former suspect and the latter disruptive

provincial, *adj.* Uncorrupted

provocateur, *n.* A French-speaking person

public, *adj.* Describing anything to do with government and the nation at large, largely hidden from the people; **public opinion**, *n.* Views of the general population, as engendered by the media and poll results

pundit, *n.* Partisan political analyst

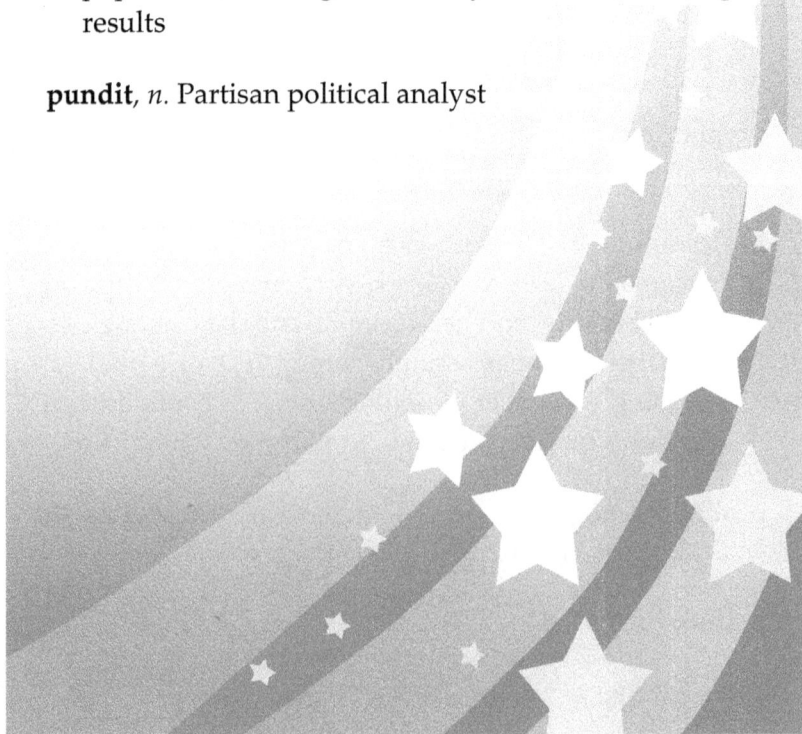

Q

qualifications, *n.* Credentials which are carefully considered when hiring a worker and disregarded when making a political appointment

QUALIFICATIONS

questionnaire, *n.* Annoying form containing questions used to pry into one's personal information for questionable purposes

quid pro quo, *n.* Latin phrase signifying that nothing is acquired for nothing

quota, *n.* An amount considered to be a fair share. For example, in baking a cake, a quota would dictate how many eggs you can use, how much sugar, how much milk, etc., the object being ingredient equity. Too many eggs would not be fair to the butter, since it would deny the butter's right to be present in sufficient relative quantity. *Ergo*, a quota represents quantity control and not quality control, ensuring that the end product will be half-baked.

quintessential, *adj.* Unnecessary

R

racist, *n.* Common epithet applied when anyone of a different ethnicity than your own disagrees with you. Since this word indicates the inability to evaluate persons non-racially, anyone using it pejoratively against a member of another race is by definition himself a racist.

radical, *adj.* **1.** Bold, forward-looking **2.** Old hat

radical, *n.* **1.** A person whose ideas are untried and therefore not invalid **2.** A person whose ideas have been tried and found invalid

reality, *n.* **1.** Anything seen on television, excepting, of course, so-called "reality shows" **2.** The opposite of an opponent's assessment

recant, *v .t.* To take back your erroneous statements after being excoriated for them

reception, *n.* A social affair at which an honored person is greeted by a "receiving" line, although just what is being given and what is being received, and by whom, is not always clear

recommendation, *n.* Advice, which is either in the form of a request, a suggestion or a demand, depending on the rank of the recommender *vis-à-vis* that of the recipient.

reconciliation, *n.* In accounting, altering a calculation to match what is actual. In Congress, altering a rule to match what is expedient

reconsideration, *n.* A second look resulting in no change of opinion

recount, *n.* Process after an election by which you discover more ballots marked for your candidate

recovery, *n.* Process of getting over a financial recession, clinical depression, illness, hangover or, more typically, all of these simultaneously

red flag, *n.* Ignored warning of impending disaster

red herring, *n.* An important matter highly germane to an issue, therefore deemed fishy by detractors

red-handed, *adj.* The worst way of being caught. It is somewhat better to be caught with "one's hands in the cookie jar" or even "with one's pants down," although it may be argued that the absolute worst way of being caught is on video tape.

redistribution of wealth, *n.* A misnomer for "distribution of wealth," since wealth is never distributed in the first place, but earned. Distribution of wealth is best defined by the oft-quoted phrase "from each according to his success, to each according to his failure."

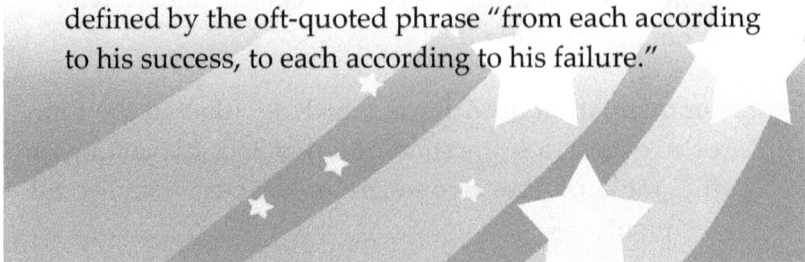

referendum, *n.* A device of governance whereby the electorate can vote on an issue directly, as opposed to voting for representatives who promise to vote one way on the issue but once elected vote the opposite way

reform, *n.* **1.** A complete change, always initially assumed to be a good thing. **2.** The repeal of an earlier reform

repeal, *v. t.* The vain hope of the opposition when a bill they fought vigorously against is passed. The percentage of laws which have been repealed is too infinitesimal to be calculated, but the existence of the word at least makes the prospect seem at least possible.

report, *n.* Damaging document

Republican, *n.* **1.** A conservative member of the Republican Party **2.** A liberal member of the Republican Party **3.** Émigré from the Soviet Union. The first true Republican president was Abraham Lincoln, and the last was Ronald Reagan. Republicans like quoting the Constitution and obstructing Democrats, and are often seen driving large fuel-inefficient cars while listening to Rush Limbaugh on the radio. Some Republicans frown upon littering and shouting, while others fail to heed these guidelines. While the Democratic party is widely considered the party of the workers, there are also, surprisingly, many Republicans who work. Some, it is rumored, are even union members, but this cannot be certified, since they would be expulsed if discovered. In a similar way there are also no known Republican teachers or professors. Many Republicans believe in original sin, but they often contend that sins of Democrats are even more original.

reputation, *n.* The regard in which others hold you, which is likely not very high, but nevertheless to be protected

respect, with all due, *adv.* Phrase used to inoculate the speaker from the insult which follows it, as "With all due respect, you are a filthy stinking idiot!"

revolution, *n.* Formerly, the rapid overturning of an unpopular government for a more desirable government. Presently, the rapid overturning of an unpopular government for another unpopular government

right, *n.* Privilege; **Constitutional right**, An entitlement which somehow got left out of the document, *i.e.* right to privacy, right to home ownership, right to healthcare, right to paid vacations, etc.

RINO, *n.* Democrat skull wearing a Republican hat

risky scheme, *n.* Innovation proposed by the other party

rugged individualist, *n.* Strongly constituted loner; *antonym:* Weakly constituted conformist

rumor, *n.* Fact

RUGGED INDIVIDUALIST

S

sabotage, *v. t.* Suggest an alternative or introduce a new fact

salvo, *n.* Remark intended to wound; **opening salvo**, *(debate)* Shot across the bow; test of an opponent's disposition to retaliate

sanction, *v. t.* **1.** To condone **2.** To express a torrent of disapproval by turning off the water

satellite, *n.* A country out on a limb and tethered by a noose, which must comply or be hung out to dry

scandal, *n.* An incident involving the outrageous, shameful behavior of an opponent

scapegoat, *n.* Person usually guilty thus easily blamed for crimes of others

scare tactic, *n.* The threatening of utter doom if someone doesn't vote for your proposal, your bill or yourself. Popular dark scenarios which can be painted include: Taxes will be raised. Jobs will be lost. Babies will not get their milk. An epidemic will take thousands. The price of gasoline will quadruple. A species will become extinct (particularly cute animals, such as pandas or prairie dogs). No one will be safe in their homes. We will never again see... (insert some commonplace item) ...as *we now know it.*

scholar, *n.* One who has been isolated in a college for a longer time than non-scholars and thus feels more qualified to express an opinion. It is always wise to speak loudly in the presence of scholars in order to be heard, since, once they get started, there is no stopping them. Scholars sometimes make good political candidates due to their ability to affect a serious tone, use big words and thereby impress the masses that they are highly intelligent; however, once elected they never make good administrators since they can't stop theorizing and pontificating long enough to actually do something. (*See* academic)

self-esteem, *n.* Overestimation of oneself, the development of which is modern education's highest goal

senior, *adj.* **1.** Superior to, as in "senior officer" **2.** Older than, as in "senior to" **3.** Superior to and older than, as in "senior citizen"

senior, *n.* **1.** Irrelevant person who offers advice and clips coupons **2.** Person who has experienced more of life's folly than most

separation of church and state, *n.* The joining of anti-church and state

separation of powers, *n.* Constitutional provision to keep divisions of government apart, so as to avoid physical altercations

Seven Deadly Sins, *n.* In political terms, the following: **1. Modesty** – Humble candidates finish last. Committing modesty is political surrender

71

2. Candor – Forthrightness, even as a tactic, is a suicidal practice.

3. Clarity – Ignoring the virtues of obfuscation and circumlocution arms your opponents.

4. Courage – Heroes lose.

5. Generosity – Giving a rival the benefit of the doubt, or anything else, betrays weakness.

6. Sincerity – To be strictly avoided, in favor of the *appearance* of sincerity, a virtue.

7. Brevity – A grave evil; the more you say, the more difficult for others to determine your position and thus open the door to criticism

sexual equality, *n.* Feminization

shakedown, *n.* Extraction of financial fruit by shaking the money tree. Shakedowns once depended upon an exploitable weakness of the victim, such as implication in a crime or scandal, the revealing of which could be threatened. In the present age, however, one need merely accuse the prospective target of harboring unwholesome thoughts, such as racism, homophobia, antifeminism, etc. Thus it can be seen that political correctness has happily proved a great boon to the extortionist's profession!

shame, *n.* State or quality of feeling a disgrace or indignity, an irrelevant word in the public arena since politicians don't know the meaning of it

simple majority, *n.* A majority of simpletons. Most of the members of Congress, as contrasted with the complex minority

skeptic, *n.* Disaster's warning light

slave, *n.* Under communism, a capitalist; under capitalism, a communist; in Great Britain, anyone not British (*See* "Rule Britannia")

slippery slope, *n.* A difficult hill to climb. Opponents of a new measure often warn that its adoption will open the door to all sorts of misfortunes and "set us on a slippery slope," to ever greater disasters, assuming erroneously that we are currently at the top of the hill, which is never the case – but then, things could always be worse.

slogan, *n.* Identifying catch phrase for a political campaign, to which much thought and attention is given, since an election's outcome largely depends on which candidate has the best. Richard M. Nixon had great success with "In your heart you know he's right," for example. "Tippecanoe and Tyler Too" is still remembered for its rhythmic ring. Good words to consider using in a slogan include: Future, Tomorrow, Building, Better, Honesty, Fight and Trust. Words to avoid: Yesterday, Past, Stupid, Careless, Fragile, Cheat, Slippery, Drunken and Failure. Also, it is always undesirable to be half-hearted with slogans. "The Candidate Who Doesn't Suck," would not appeal, likewise "Not As Bad As The Last Guy" or "Worth A Try."

smear, *v.* Describe

soapbox, *n.* Small platform for an unimportant or short speaker

soccer mom, *n*. Stereotypical woman who might vote either way, therefore courted by all

social justice, *n*. **1.** Result of everyone getting what they lack, *i.e.* enrichment of the poor, impoverishment of the rich, heightening of the short, shortening of the tall, etc. **2.** The eradicator of class envy

Social Security, *n*. A system of motivating older workers to retire and still collect a monthly check, in order to open jobs for younger workers who are then taxed in order to support the retired

socialism, *n*. A system of government in which the state persistently taxes rich employers and gives to poor workers until such time as there is nobody left to tax and nobody left to work for, with the possible exception of Walmart

source, *n*. Journalist's friend in the government who can't keep a secret, but expects the journalist to keep one, namely the source's identity

spin, *n*. Information in *italics*. (*See* slanted)

spy, *n*. A secret agent glorified by his own country and hanged by others

State of the Union, *n*. An annual speech by the president in which he lists the state of his personal achievements and congratulates those who have obeyed him

state, *n.* Geographical section of the United States with its own board of tourism. When motoring across America, one knows when one is in a new state by signs at the roadside and the sudden prevalence of different license plates. When flying, one has no way to tell, unless the pilot announces a new state. States also have different laws, especially those dealing with speed limits and the drinking age – the main reason why it is so important to know what state you are in. States are often grouped together, such as "New England" states, "Midwestern" states, "Gulf" states, "wet" states, "dry" states, "red" states, "blue" states etc., complicating things even further. Each state has its own state flower, state bird, state song and state governor, but most inhabitants don't even know these facts about their home state let alone other states. Also, it's a good thing to memorize the capital cities of each state, in case you ever appear on *Jeopardy*; **red state**, *n.* State in which most people know someone currently in the military; **blue state**, *n.* State in which most people know someone currently in jail; **purple state**, *n.* State in which one might know a person not in one's own party, but not very well

statement, *n.* Apology or excuse issued by an official after a fiasco

states' rights, *n.* Originally, left-over powers not granted to the federal government which fall to the states. Currently, powers not granted to the federal government which fall to the federal government

statesman, *n.* Dead politician

statism, *n.* Globalism's migraine

statistic, *n.* **1.** Datum selected to support an argument or prove a point and unselected if unhelpful **2.** Victim of a career-killing scandal

status quo, *n.* The present, unchangeable condition

stimulus, *n.* In time of economic recession, free cash provided by legislators in order to stimulate campaign coffers and buy votes

stock exchange, *n.* A legal betting parlor where fortunes can be made, most notably by brokers and consultants

strategery, *n.* Word inadvertently coined by George W. Bush, meaning the science of strateging, indulged in by strategers

straw vote, *n.* Preliminary poll taken to influence the outcome of the final vote, based on the proposition that in the majority is the place to be

study, *n.* Fact-finding tactic **government study**, Course of action taken in order to avoid making a timely decision

subsidy, *n.* Government handout given to restrain the private sector from developing independence from government

stump speech, *n.* A candidate's standard address repeated in every town on the campaign trail, hence any clichéd oratory

STUMP SPEECH

suburbia, *n.* A nondescript zone, neither urban nor rural, typified by nondescript voters, neither very right nor very left, fish nor fowl, hence a popular area

summit, *n.* A meeting, originally in a mountainous setting, at which the high and mighty exchange niceties, proposals, state secrets, etc.

Supreme Court, *n.* The second legislative branch of government, whose nine members are not elected, but appointed according to their political agendas

suppress, *v.* Summon one's best, civic-minded efforts to eliminate the negative, hide bad news, stifle opposition, etc.

swiftboating, *n.* The releasing of a barrage of true accounts about a candidate in order to defeat his election

T

talk radio, *n.* Popular mass medium characterized by uncontrolled, hence politically incorrect, speech. (*Exception*: government-funded National Public Radio)

taxation, *n.* Theft made legal by governments

teach, *v. t.* Dominate a pupil

teachable moment, *n.* A bumbler's public fiasco which he deems "a lesson we can all learn from"

Ten Commandments, *n.* The Decalogue; Biblical laws upon which modern jurisprudence is based, generally banned from display in court houses so as not to intimidate citizens into following them

tendentious, *adj.* Not quite biased, which is not quite prejudiced, which is not quite bigoted

tenure, *n.* Lifetime employment guaranteed to college professors in order to protect them from facing the difficulties they would encounter seeking honest work

term limits, *n.* A scheme fostering more frequent changing of elected officials, so that corrupt office-holders are more quickly replaced with other corrupt office-holders

TEACH

test case, *n.* A court trial involving a crime no one has ever thought of before

textbook, *n.* Volume issued by learning institutions to shape prejudices of students

theocracy, *n.* Government by Jesuits

think tank, *n.* Egghead group engaged in communal authorship of individual views, mainly in the business of recommending

timetable, *n.* Additional feature added to an unpopular plan in order to make it more palatable by implementing it in small increments

tolerance, *n.* Benevolent acceptance of those one deems inferior

trade, *n.* International commerce beneficial to all except labor unions

tradeoff, *n.* The surrendering of something of minor value so as to acquire something of higher value while appearing to make a sacrifice

transition, *n.* The period of political war between the election of a new administration and the trashing of the previous one

transparency, *n.* Openness promised by the nominated and forgotten by the elected

treason, *n.* An act of loyalty to another country

treaty, *n.* An agreement among nations providing mutual benefits to their leaders

trial balloon, *n.* The publication of your proposed action in order to determine whether or not you favor it

trial, *n.* Legal contest to determine a defendant's likeability

truth, *n.* Whatever will be believed; *antonym:* Incredulity

two-thirds majority, *n.* A larger majority of Congress than the "simple majority" (*q. v.*), whose members have lost only one-third of their senses

U

unconstitutional, *adj.* Describing laws which do not conform to the Constitution, *i.e.* some state laws and most all federal laws

unemployment, *n.* A condition resulting from an over-abundance of workers and/or a shortage of jobs. There is no governmental solution to unemployment except reducing the number of workers or increasing the number of jobs, neither of which is possible or legal.

United Kingdom, n. The combined countries of Great Britain and Northern Ireland. U.K. citizens speak mostly English, though they are often misunderstood by Americans. The English call elevators "lifts" and trucks "lorries," and have odd spellings of common words, such as "centre," "organisation," and "tyre." They also mispronounce many words such as "lavatory" ("lava-tree") and "fortune" ("for-choon"). Nevertheless – The U. K. historically has had a special relationship with the United States, mainly because our founders were its most noted insurrectionists (with the possible exceptions of the Irish and East Indians). The United Kingdom is a parliamentary democracy but supports socialized medicine and, for old time's sake, a royal family.

United Nations, *n.* A democratic organization of author-itarian governments

United States, *n.* **1.** Separate states united by a central government. **2.** (*common error*) A central government divided up into states. Citizens of the United States of America are commonly called "Americans" *(q. v.)* and are mostly interested in pop culture developments rather than political matters.

university, *n.* A learning institution "universally" radical, liberal, Marxist, Methodist, etc.

unprecedented, *adj.* Perpetually rejected in the past

Upper West Side, *n.* New York City enclave where no one even knows a Republican. (*See* Moscow)

UNEMPLOYMENT

V

values, *n.* Prejudices; **our values**, Our party's superior moralities, as opposed to "their values," which are wrongheaded

vet, *v. t.* To uncover dirt on one's nominee before one's opponents do

vice-president, *n.* The person first in line for the world's most powerful office, whose principal qualification for selection consists of residing in the South if the presidential candidate is from the North, and vice versa

victim, *n.* One subjected to something disapproved of or painful. Designation as a victim largely depends upon the nature of the subjected. For example, some may love Wagnerian opera; others are its victims. Other things of which one may be a victim include: medical treatment, oratory, piety, advice, air travel, designer clothes and constructive criticism.

victimhood, *n.* Institutionalized sympathy for certain groups, *i.e.* the viewing of criminals as victims of poverty or the poor as victims of crime

voodoo, *n.* The nature of a rival's proposal, which, unlike your own, is filled with illogical ideas and incomeprehensible nonsense

vote, *n*. Congressional commodity the value of which is in direct proportion to the closeness of a bill's passage. A vote can be purchased in several ways: a promised allocation to one's re-election fund, pork spending in one's home state, a personal promotion or appointment, a promise to consider one's hitherto ignored proposal, etc., but never in cash, as this would be deemed unethical.

VICE PRESIDENT

W

War On Poverty, *n.* Combat operation to eliminate the indigent, declared by President Lyndon B. Johnson in 1964 and continuing to the present and beyond. The main problem with this war is that, as fast as you can eliminate the enemy, reinforcements appear.

war, *n.* **1.** The most unfortunate result of impatience **2.** The most unfortunate result of patience

wealthy, *n.* Moneyed class whose members are perpetually receiving either tax hikes or tax cuts, depending on which party currently reigns

weapons of mass destruction, *n.* Devices capable of great damage, especially to pacifists, but usually hidden and therefore not an issue

weasel, *v. t.* To back out of a statement by rewording it

welfare, *n.* Government payments to insolvent individuals or commercial enterprises

whip, *n.* Herder of congressional cattle

whipping boy, *n.* A person regularly assigned to take the credit for your idiotic ideas

whistle-stopping, *n.* Campaigning in several towns in rapid succession, often resulting in a candidate's confusion about where he is at the moment, somewhat analogous to barhopping, but with less beer

White House, *n.* A palatial residence supported by United States taxpayers so that the president may entertain monarchs, film stars and campaign donors in their accustomed style

win-win, *n.* Situation in which A wins, B wins and C loses

witch hunt, *n.* Routine investigation

wrong side of history, *n.* One's projected future location when currently outside the herd of mindless conformists

WITCH HUNT

X

X, *n.* Generation unable to sign its name

xenophobia, *n.* International prudence

Xerox, *n.* Photocopying process enabling documents of worthless nonsense or incomprehensible gibberish to be replicated *ad inflnltum*

Y

yack, *v. i. (slang)* Speak nonsense at length, hence, to a politician, to speak

yahoo, *n.* One of an opponent's constituency, as contrasted with one's own constituency, the "American people"

Yankee, *n.* Person who will not eat grits or speak slowly

Yellow Dog Democrats, *n.* Traditional Democrats, identified with the old South, originally so named because they "would rather vote for a yellow dog than a Republican." Ironically they eventually became Republicans, presumably even worse than yellow dogs.

yeoman, *n.* A really hard worker in spite of his failure

yesterday's news, *n.* Potentially compromising item revealed today, so defined in order to diminish its effect by suggesting that it is old stuff

youngster, *n.* A Congressperson under the age of sixty

youth movement, *n.* Small group of angry college students

YouTube, *n.* Internet site for posting damaging videos of your rivals

Z

zealot, *n.* One who cheers first and thinks later

zigzag, *v. i.* To go one way then another while making little headway, as in an attempt to explain to others something one doesn't understand oneself

Zionism, *n.* Belief that all Jews should leave wherever they are unless they're in Israel

zip, *v. t.* Instruction to accomplices as to what to do with their lips. (*See* collusion)

zoo, *n.* Session of Congress

ABOUT THE AUTHOR

*H*aving written two bestselling books about dogs, John Clifton turns his attention in this volume to politics, another pet (!) topic of his. With sincere apologies to Webster, Funk, Wagnall and all serious lexicographers, John presents his uniquely twisted definitions of political terms you either (erroneously) thought you already knew, admittedly don't know, or never even wanted to know.

John's life has spanned many careers, since he never knew exactly what he wanted to be when he grew up, and was still in this quandary well beyond middle age. That's why, while best known as a musical theater composer/lyricist, Clifton has also at various times in his life been a commercial artist, Broadway pianist, music educator, book designer, computer teacher, patented inventor, Web site designer, and obviously, author.

John is a graduate of Carnegie Mellon University and has lived on New York's Upper West Side since 1962, but would not like this to be held against him. His wife is writer Josée Clerens, a native of Belgium, a country in Europe.

For complete information or to email the author an excoriating note, visit him online at *JohnClifton.net* .

ORDER FORM

To order additional copies of this book, simply fill in this form and mail with payment.

Please send me _____ copies of *The Forbidden Political Dictionary*

How many copies?	**Cost** ($9.95 + $2.00 S/H **per copy**)	Total Enclosed (Check or Money Order Only)
▼	x $11.95	= ▼

Ship via USPS Mail.

<u>Note</u>: **Domestic (US) orders only.** For foreign orders, please purchase online at *www.ForbiddenDictionary.com*

PLEASE PRINT CLEARLY:

Full Name	
Address 1	
Address 2	
City	State
Zip Code	
Email	
Telephone (day): [   ] [   ]
Area   Number

Send to:
Foley Square Books
Direct Sales
P. O. Box 20548, Park West Station
New York, NY 10025